Collins



# Cherry Blossoms

## Mathematics

### LKG

FS2

SERIES EDITOR: RANI THIPPAVAZZULA

## Student + Teacher

**a** animations

**ilt** instructor-led tutorials

**ia** activities

**w** worksheets

audio

**g** games

**v** videos

## Teacher-only

**lp** lesson plans

**w** worksheets

**tn** teacher's notes

**ak** answer keys

# Preface

**Cherry Blossoms** provides graded, age-appropriate learning opportunities targeting holistic skill development for children in the age group of 3 years to 8 years. The series aligns with the vision outlined in the National Education Policy, 2020 for early years. It spreads across five levels, Nursery (Foundational Stage 1) to Class 2 (Foundational Stage 5). The books use a combination of hands-on activities, frequent recapitulation and child-friendly artwork to facilitate learning.

The series comprises **40 books** and spans **English**, **Maths**, **General Awareness**, and **Art and Craft**. The series comes bundled with a **workbook** for each subject and a book of **rhymes** and **stories** for Foundational Stage 1 to 3.

This series integrates the essence of **NIPUN Bharat** guidelines, which extensively deal with Foundational Literacy and Numeracy. The series aims to motivate learners to read independently, to improve their vocabulary, number sense and spatial understanding. The **Foundational Literacy and Numeracy (FLN)** skills include the skills for developing their critical thinking, logical reasoning and creative skills, as well as the skills to enhance their ability to express themselves both verbally and in writing.

Cherry Blossoms Teacher Support Materials include:

**Teacher's Resource Books:** Comprises stories, activity banks, classroom management and assessment guidelines

**Multimedia eBook:** Consists of animations, audio, video, slide shows, and interactive exercises

**Print-ready Worksheets:** Additional worksheets for practice and reinforcement, present in the digital support

**Digital Flashcards:** Flashcards with embedded sounds and animations for letter formation and letter-sound association

**Animations and Songs:** Animated stories and rhymes set to tune

**Interactive Games:** Interactivities to reinforce concepts in a fun and engaging manner

**A note on the activity banks (included in the Teacher's Manuals)**

The activity banks comprise hands-on activities that will help children develop the requisite skills to attain age-appropriate learning goals. In keeping with Howard Gardener's theory of multiple intelligences, the activity banks include options and variations that enable teachers to provide a planned cycle of experiences and opportunities, which foster each type of intelligence, to every child in their classrooms. The activity banks equip teachers to use the strengths of children as a means of complementing their less developed areas by valuing and nurturing the inherent abilities of the children.

**Rani Thippavazzula,** former Academic Director, Ravindra Bharathi Group is an eminent educationist with over two decades of experience in teaching, administration and curriculum design and development. As an Academic Advisor for chain schools pan India, she is proficient in developing learning products and is a specialist in Differentiated Instruction, Enterprise Education and Early Childhood Education.

## Learning and Development During the Early Years

The early years are the most significant years for growth, development and learning. During this period, children need adequate opportunities for stimulating experiences as these favourably affect various learning abilities. Learning experiences, when chosen and planned properly, fuel the innate curiosity of children, and stimulate their thought processes.

The goal of learning during the early years is to enhance the all-round development of personality and to inculcate healthy attitudes, life skills and good values. Creative play, well thought-out games and developmentally appropriate activities help children develop the necessary skills to achieve these goals. The skills that children need to acquire can broadly be categorized as:

**Motor:**
Motor skills pertain not only to gross motor activities like walking and jumping but also include fine motor activities like the ability to hold a pencil and write. The development of motor skills is facilitated through several graded activities.

**Personal, Social and Emotional:**
Personal, social and emotional development, necessary for the overall personality development of children, is achieved using a combination of hands-on activities, role plays and thought-provoking stories and rhymes.

**Linguistic:**
The ability to listen, speak, read and write is critical to success in formal learning environments.

**Mathematical:**
The development of mathematical ideas and concepts is important at this stage since children will continue to build on this learning for most of their years of schooling.

**Knowledge and Understanding of the World:**
This is achieved through activities that enable children to explore their surroundings at home and in the school, and interact with the people that they see around them.

**Health and Safety:** The idea of health and safety is introduced through activities, stories and retelling of real-life experiences to encourage children to focus on health and well-being.

**Creative:**
Creative skills are developed through a host of activities involving art, craft, painting, roleplays, etc.

**Logical and Rational Thinking:**
Activities that involve simple puzzles, pattern-completion and visual discrimination help children to develop logical and rational thinking skills.

# Contents

# WALKTHROUGH

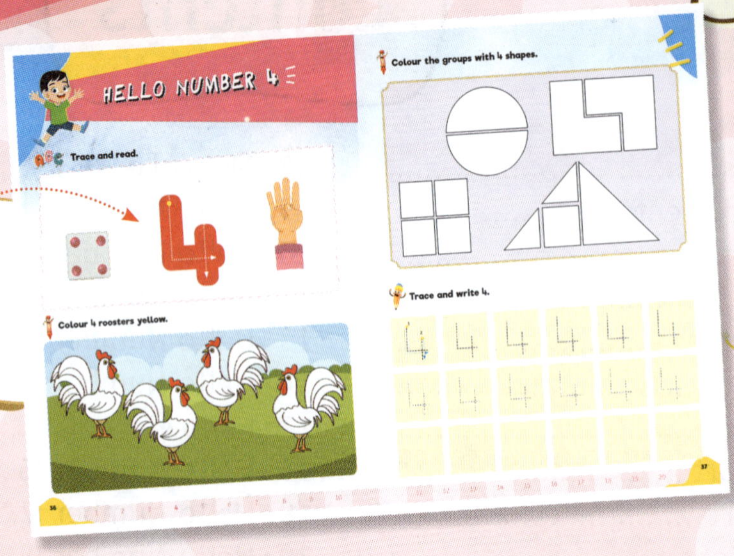


Number formation with pattern tracing

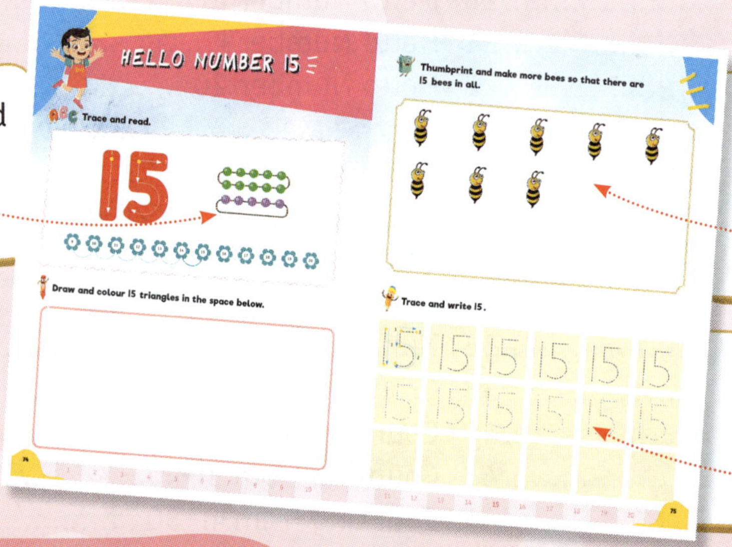


Counting beyond 10 continued using groups of 10

Exercise to strengthen number-value association

Pattern tracing for fine motor development

Two-page spreads have been used to introduce numbers 1-20. The emphasis is on improving number recognition and strengthening number-value association through a variety of exercises. The teacher's manual includes stories, which can be used to accomplish these goals.

New concepts introduced through short rhymes to make it fun for little learners, followed by practice pages for reinforcement.

Frequent revision pages in various formats included to reinforce learning.

A variety of activities included to support the development of logical and rational thinking skills.

Activities such as spot the difference help develop visual discrimination and observation skills.

# DIRECTIONS

Trace and colour the lines. Start at the red dot (•).

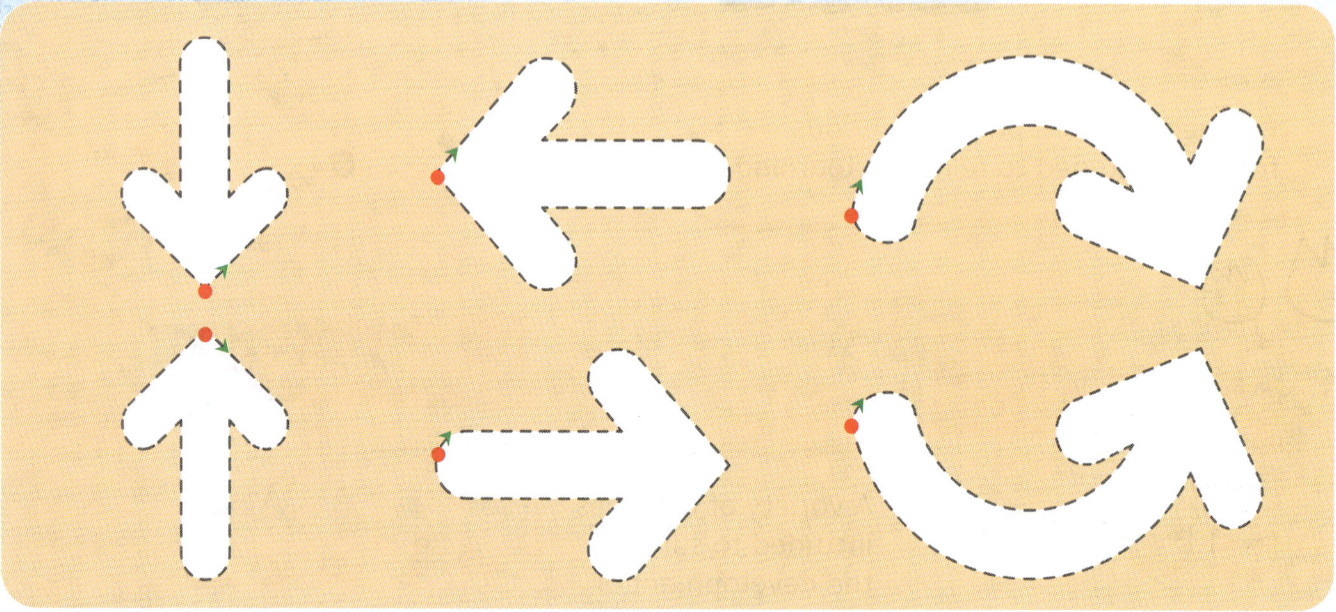

Ring the children at the top of the ladder.

# SAME-DIFFERENT

**Look at these pictures.**

same    same    different    different

**Cross (✗) the different one.**

# NEAR-FAR

Look carefully at this picture.

## Look the picture on the left. Tick (✓) the correct picture.

Things near me

Things far away from me

## Match the things that go together.

# IN–OUT

**Look at these pictures.**

in

out

**Cross out (✗) the animals in the farm.**

# OPEN-CLOSE

**Look at these pictures.**

open

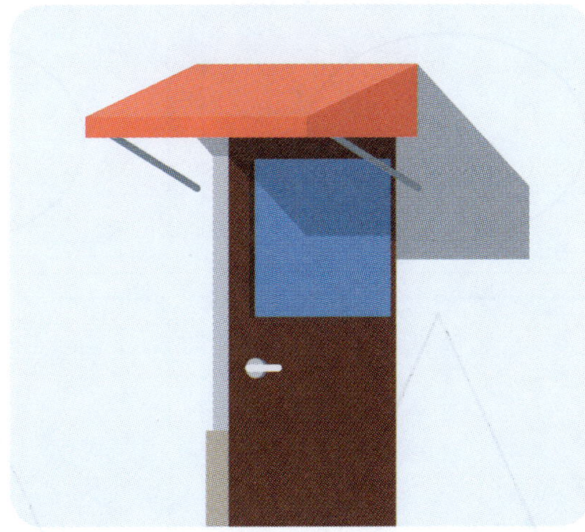

closed

**Colour the open boxes. Cross out (✗) the closed boxes.**

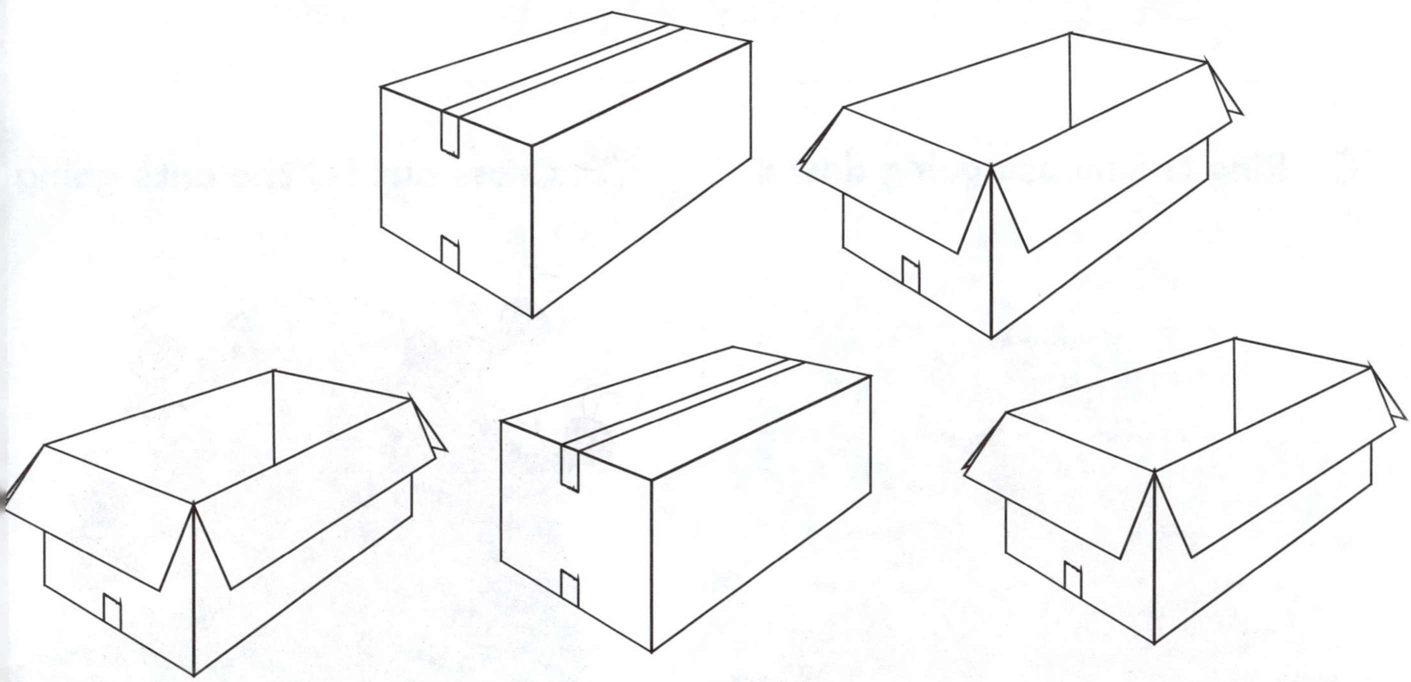

# I KNOW!

Colour the different picture in each row.

Ring the mouse going down.

Cross out (✗) the ants going

# I KNOW!

Colour the different tree green.

Paste stickers of birds away from the tree. Colour the open box under the tree.

# I KNOW!

**Take the rabbits to the carrots.**

Use  to go ↓ ,  to go ← ,  to go → ; and  to go ↑ .

# BIG-SMALL

Look at these pictures.

big small small big

Tick (✓) the big picture in each group.

# LONG-SHORT

Look at these pictures.

short

long

Tick (✓) the long object. Cross out (✗) the short object.

# TALL-SHORT

Look at these pictures.

tall

short

Colour the tall tree and the short boy.

# HEAVY-LIGHT

**Look at these pictures.**

heavy

light

**Thumbprint the light objects.**

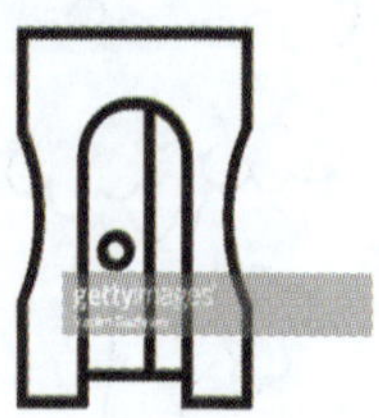

# THICK – THIN

Look at these pictures.

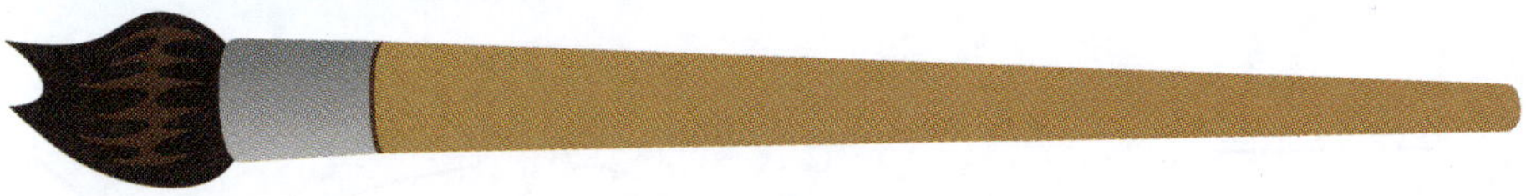

thick

thin

Tick (✓) the thick object. Cross out (✗) the thin object.

 ☐  ☐

 ☐  ☐

 ☐  ☐

# I KNOW!

Circle the short picture.

Colour the long picture.

Draw a smile on the thick face. Colour it yellow.

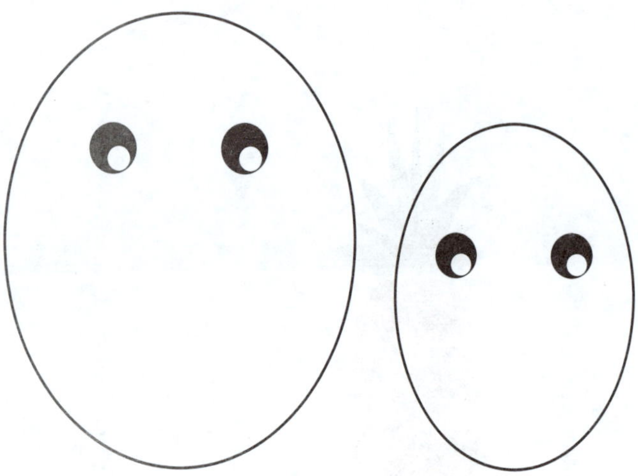

Colour the tall picture.

# I KNOW!

**Tick (✓) the heavy object. Colour the light object.**

**Colour the big toy.**

**Draw a small gift.**

big small

# I KNOW!

Tick (✓) the correct picture.

tall

short

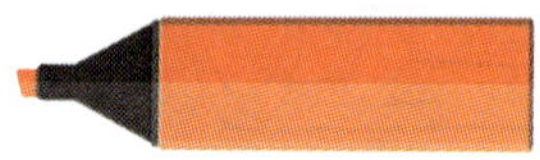

long

heavy

# FUN TIME

**Cross (✗) the odd one out.**

# SHAPES

Hello! I am a triangle.

Hello! I am a circle.

Hello! I am a square.

**Count and write the number of each shape.**

Use the same colour to colour the same shapes.

Match the two parts of the same object.

# SHAPES

Hello! I am an oval. Hello! I am a rectangle. Hello! I am a diamond.

**Match the picture to the correct shape.**

| | |
|---|---|
| rectangle • | •  |
| oval • | •  |
| diamond • | •  |

**Paste stickers of shapes to complete the picture.**

# HELLO NUMBER 1

**Trace and read.**

**Colour 1 bird.**

**Cross out (✗) the nest with 1 egg.**

**Trace and write 1.**

1

11 12 13 14 15 16 17 18 19 20

# HELLO NUMBER 2

**Trace and read.**

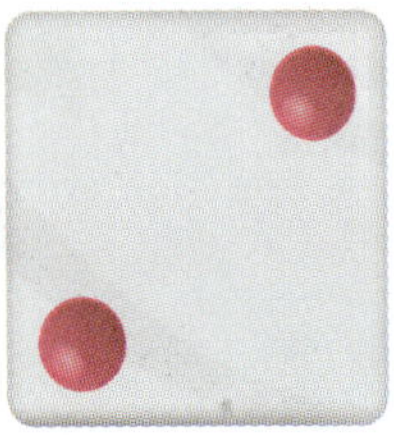

**Colour 2 cows.**

Draw 2 horns on each cow.

Trace and write 2.

# HELLO NUMBER 3

**Trace and read.**

**Colour the picture. Draw 3 nuts for each squirrel.**

Draw and colour 3 leaves on the branch.

Trace and write 3.

# HELLO NUMBER 4

Trace and read.

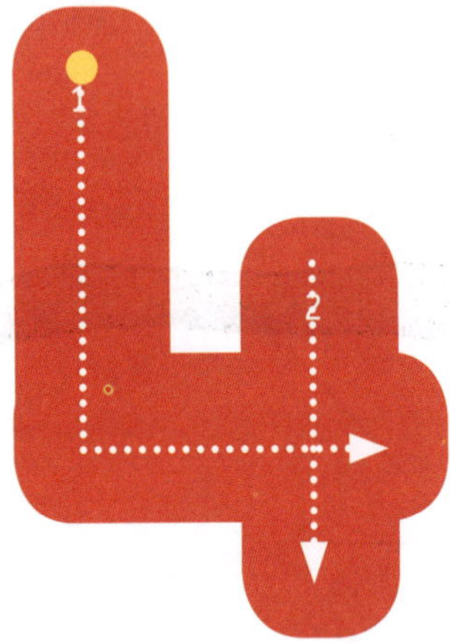

Colour 4 roosters yellow.

Colour the groups with 4 shapes.

Trace and write 4.

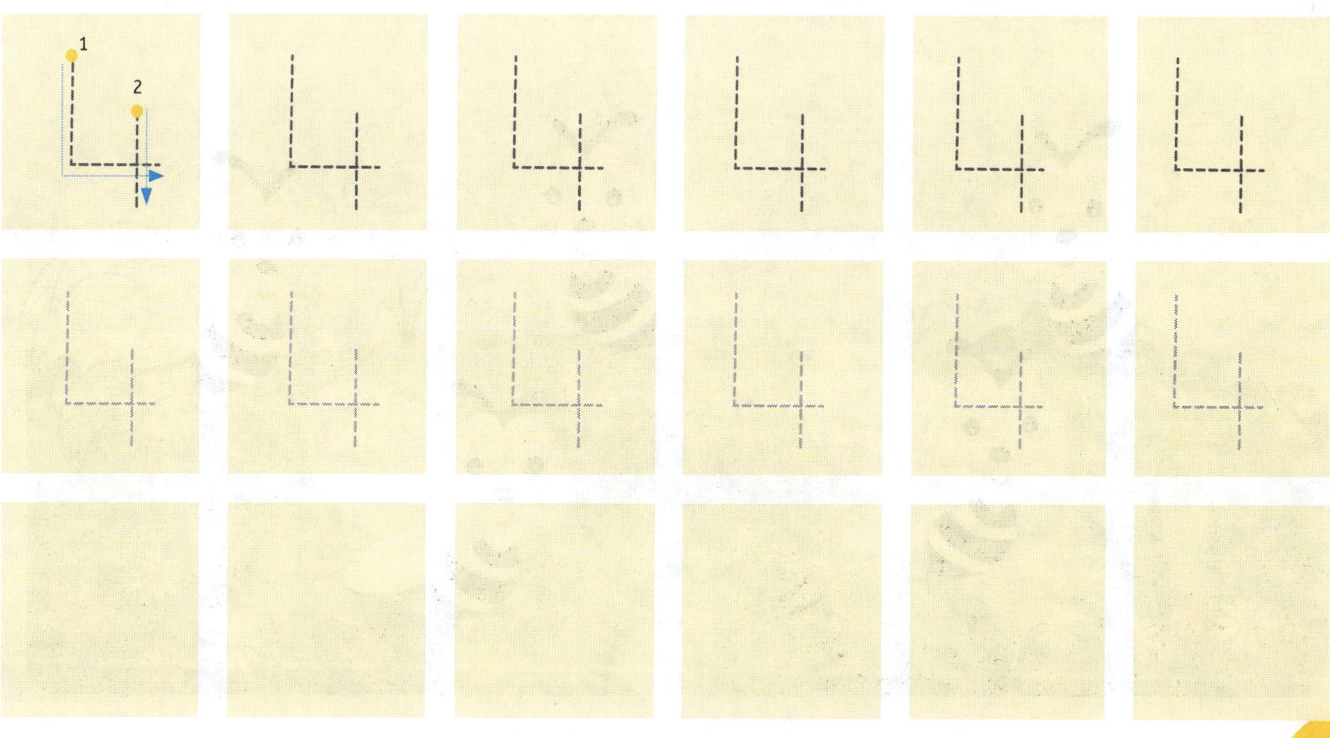

# HELLO NUMBER 5

Trace and read.

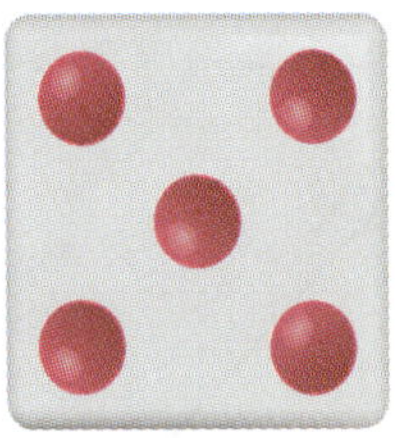

Trace 5 bees. Colour them.

Cotton print to make 5 flowers. Use any colour you like.

Trace and write 5.

# I KNOW!

**Match the same numbers.**

1 2 3 4 5

5 4 2 3 1

**Match the numbers with the same number of dots.**

2
5
4
1
3

# I KNOW!

Match the numbers to the same number of fingers.

| 3 | 5 | 4 | 1 | 2 |
|---|---|---|---|---|

Paste the correct number of stickers.

| | |
|---|---|
| 5 |  |
| 2 |  |
| 1 |  |
| 3 |  |
| 4 |  |

11 12 13 14 15 16 17 18 19 20

# I KNOW!

Trace and write the numbers.

# FUN TIME

**Spot 5 differences between these pictures.**

# HELLO NUMBER 6

Trace and read.

Draw 6 spots on the frog. Colour the frog.

## Draw 6 legs for each insect.

## Trace and write 6.

# HELLO NUMBER 7

Trace and read.

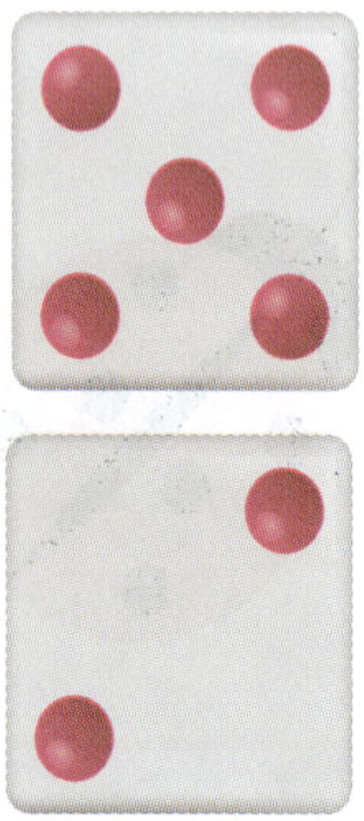

Join the dots to complete the picture and colour it.

**Draw 7 sugar cubes for the ant. Colour the ant.**

**Trace and write 7.**

# HELLO NUMBER 8

**Trace and read.**

**Paste stickers of 8 eggs in the nest.**

## Draw and colour 8 worms.

## Trace and write 8.

# HELLO NUMBER 9

Trace and read.

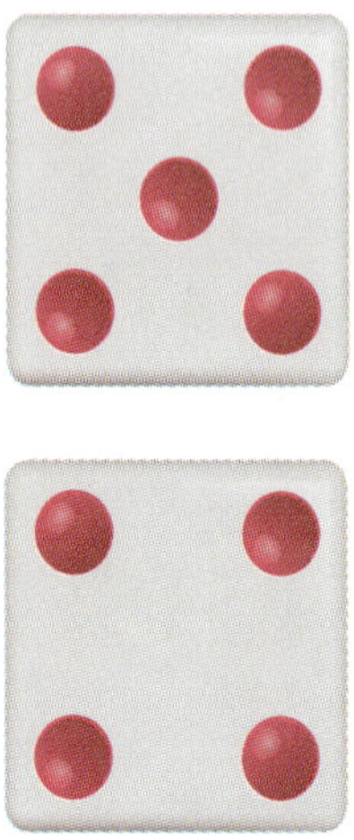

Draw and colour 9 bananas for the elephants.

## Cross out (✗) 9 elephants in the picture.

## Trace and write 9.

# HELLO NUMBER 0

**Trace and read.**

**Cross (✗) 0 stars in the picture.**

## Draw 0 cherries on the ice creams.

## Trace and write 0.

1

# HELLO NUMBER 10

Trace and read.

Draw 10 stripes on the tiger. Colour it.

**Draw and colour 10 boxes.**

**Trace and write 10.**

10 10 10 10 10 10

10 10 10 10 10 10

# I KNOW!

Match the same numbers.

| 9 | 8 | 7 | 10 | 6 |
|---|---|---|---|---|

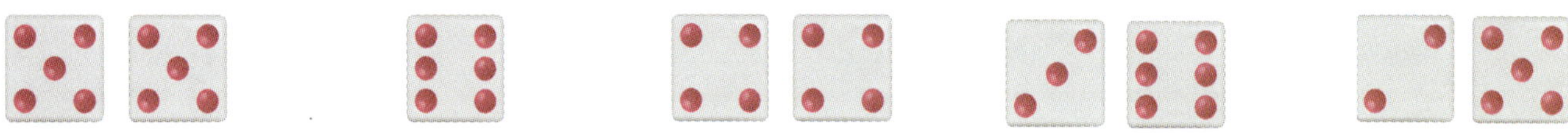

Paste the correct number of stickers.

6 

9 

10 

8 

7 

# I KNOW!

**Match the numbers to the same number of fingers.**

| | |
|---|---|
| 9 |  |
| 8 | 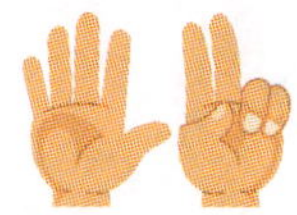 |
| 6 | 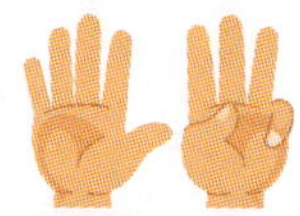 |
| 10 | 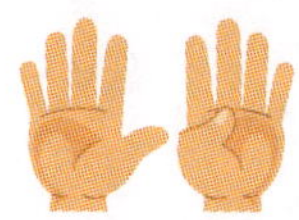 |
| 7 | 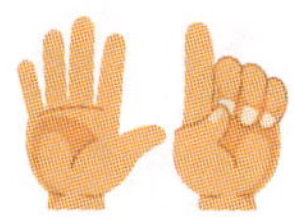 |

**Match the stars with the same number of dots.**

| | |
|---|---|
| ★★★★★★★★★★ |  |
| ★★★★★★★★ | 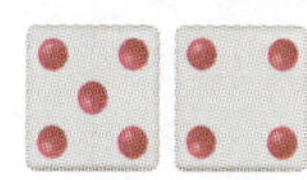 |
| ★★★★★★ | 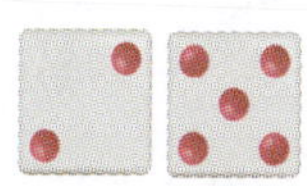 |
| ★★★★★★★★★ | 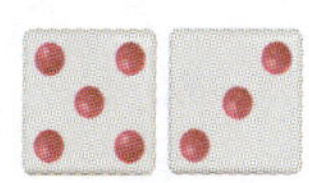 |
| ★★★★★★★ |  |

# I KNOW!

Trace and write the numbers.

# I KNOW!

**Fill in the missing numbers to take the ant home.**

# COUNT AND WRITE

Count and write the correct number.

# BACKWARD COUNTING 10-1

**Count backwards and write numbers from 10 to 1.**
**Help the frog jump on each number and reach the ant.**

# BEFORE-AFTER-BETWEEN

**Sing.**

Mr. Engine number 9,
You have 3 bogies so fine!
Red comes before the blue bogey
Green comes after, chugging slowly.
Blue is between red and green,
You are the best I have seen!

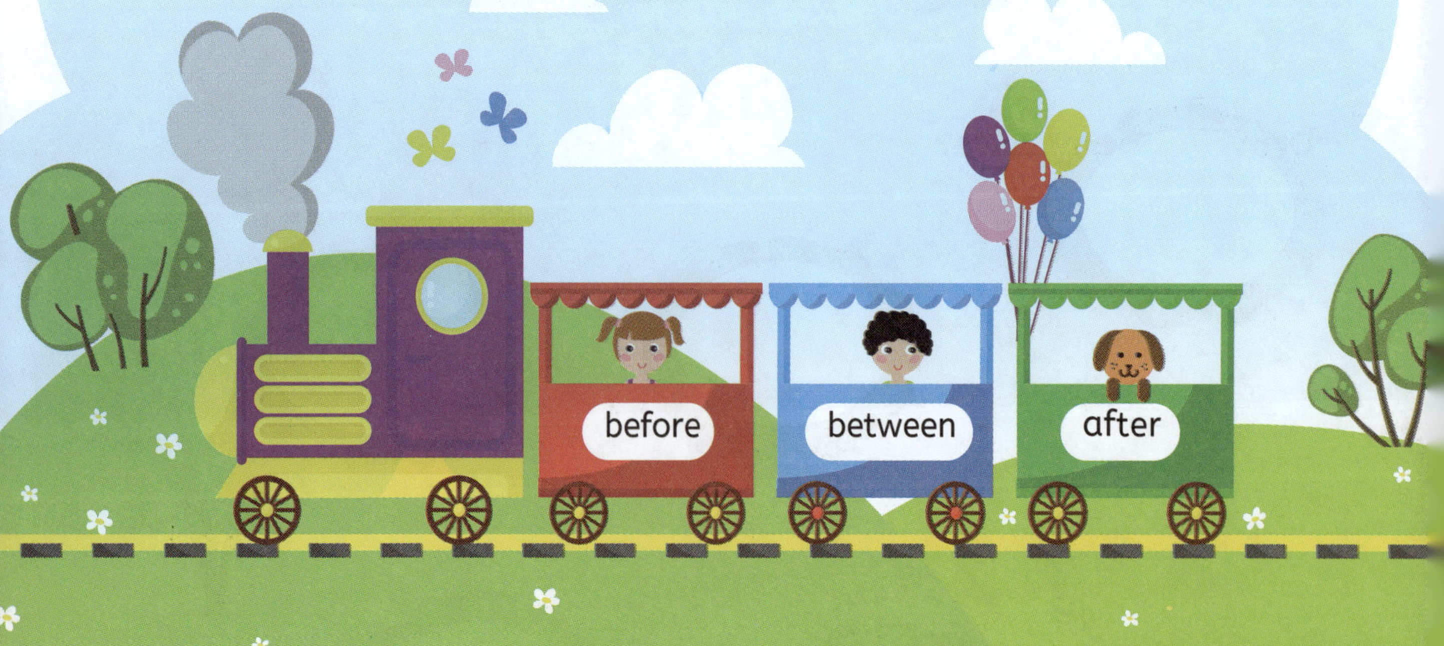

**Cross out (✗) the bogey that comes between the  and .**

**Ring the bogey that comes before .**

**Draw a bogey after .**

# BEFORE-AFTER-BETWEEN

Write the numbers that come just before.

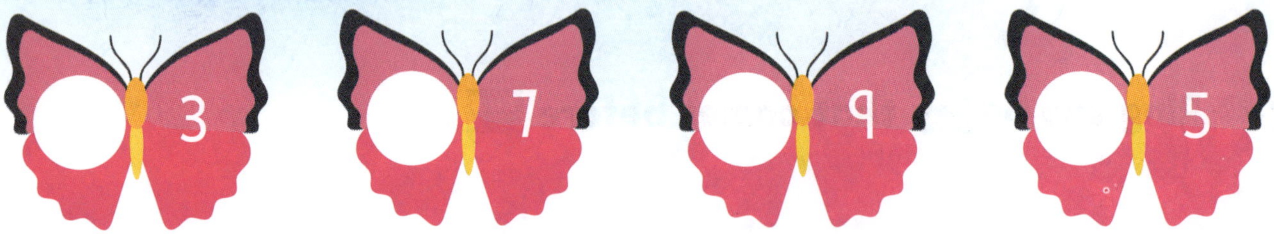


Write the numbers that come just after.

Write the missing number between the given numbers.

# MORE-LESS

Tick (✓) the vase with more flowers.

Colour the plate with less toffees.

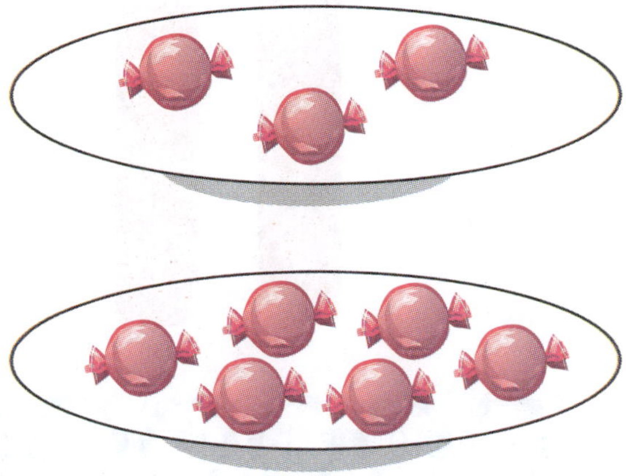

Count and write the number of each.

# HELLO NUMBER 11

**Trace and read.**

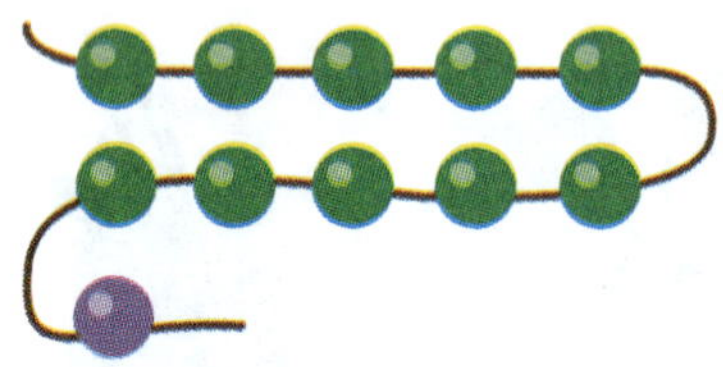

9 10 11 12 13 14 15 16 17 18 19 20

**Draw and colour 11 pencils in the space below.**

Draw more crayons so that there are 11 crayons in all.

Trace and write 11.

# HELLO NUMBER 12

Trace and read.

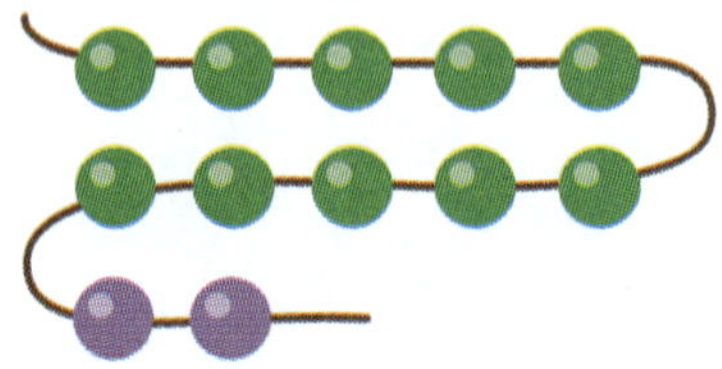

9 10 11 12 13 14 15 16 17 18 19 20

Draw and colour 12 gifts in the space below.

Draw more circles so that there are 12 circles in all.

Trace and write 12.

# HELLO NUMBER 13

**Trace and read.**

13

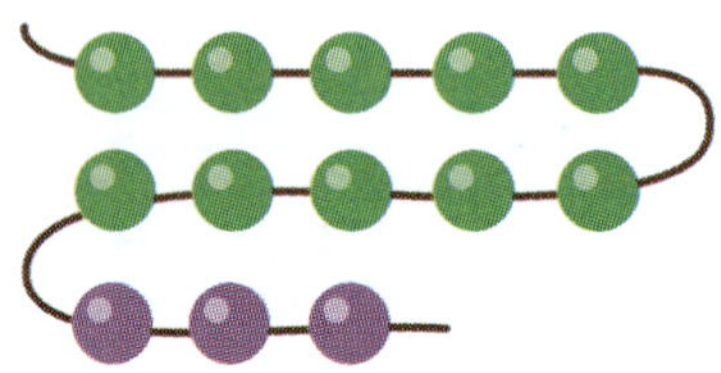

9 10 11 12 13 14 15 16 17 18 19 20

**Draw and colour 13 cakes in the space below.**

Draw more stars so that there are 13 stars in all.

Trace and write 13.

# HELLO NUMBER 14

**Trace and read.**

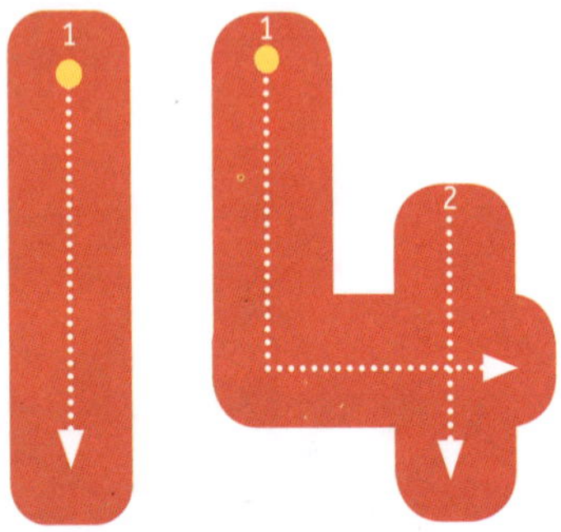


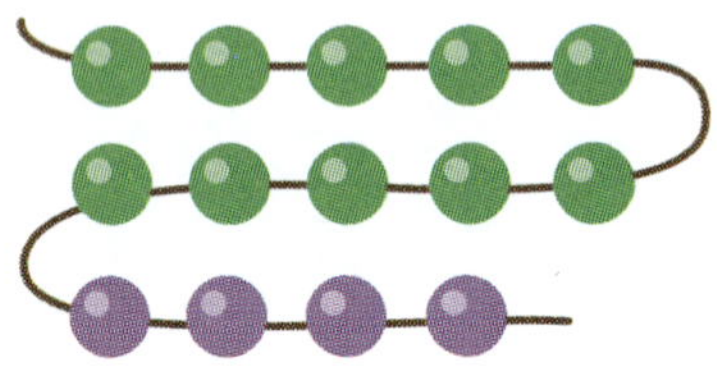

**Draw and colour 14 candles in the space below.**

Use vegetable printing to make more flowers so that there are 14 flowers in all.

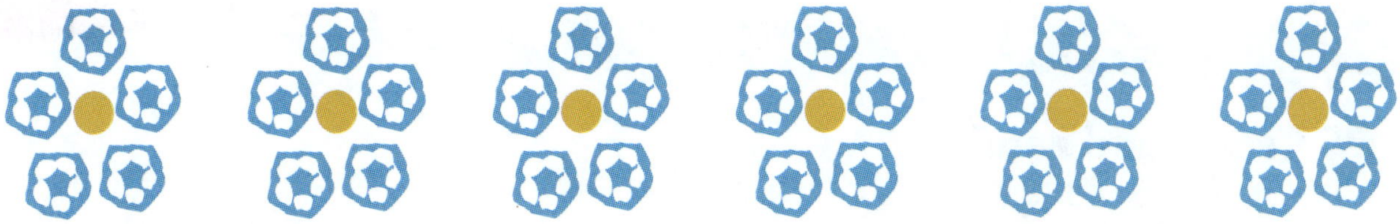

Trace and write 14.

| 14 | 14 | 14 | 14 | 14 | 14 |
|---|---|---|---|---|---|
| 14 | 14 | 14 | 14 | 14 | 14 |
| | | | | | |

# HELLO NUMBER 15

Trace and read.

15

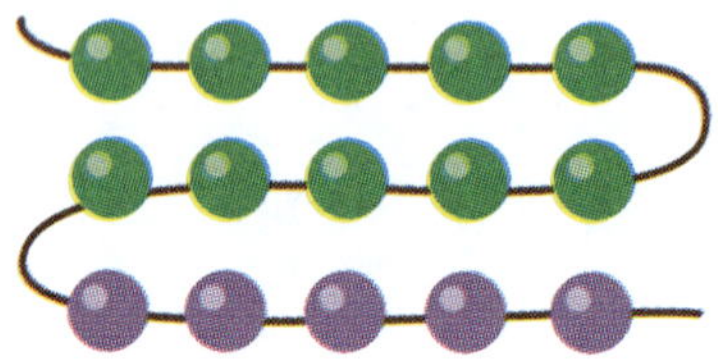

9 10 11 12 13 14 15 16 17 18 19 20

Draw and colour 15 triangles in the space below.

Thumbprint and make more bees so that there are 15 bees in all.

Trace and write 15.

# I KNOW!

**Match the same numbers.**

| | |
|---|---|
| 14 • | • 11 |
| 13 • | • 12 |
| 15 • | • 14 |
| 11 • | • 13 |
| 12 • | • 15 |

**Match the numbers to the correct number of objects.**

13 • • 

11 • • 

15 • • 

12 • • 

14 • • 

# I KNOW!

**Trace and write the numbers.**

| | | | | |
|---|---|---|---|---|
| 11 | 11 | 11 | 11 | |
| 12 | 12 | 12 | 12 | |
| 13 | 13 | 13 | 13 | |
| 14 | 14 | 14 | 14 | |
| 15 | 15 | 15 | 15 | |

# HELLO NUMBER 16

**Trace and read.**

16

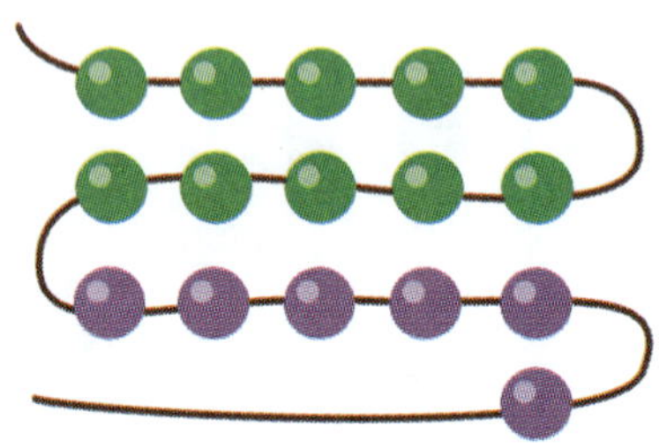

9 10 11 12 13 14 15 16 17 18 19 20

**Draw and colour 16 squares in the space below.**

**Print with a cotton bud to make more shoots so that there are 16 shoots in all.**

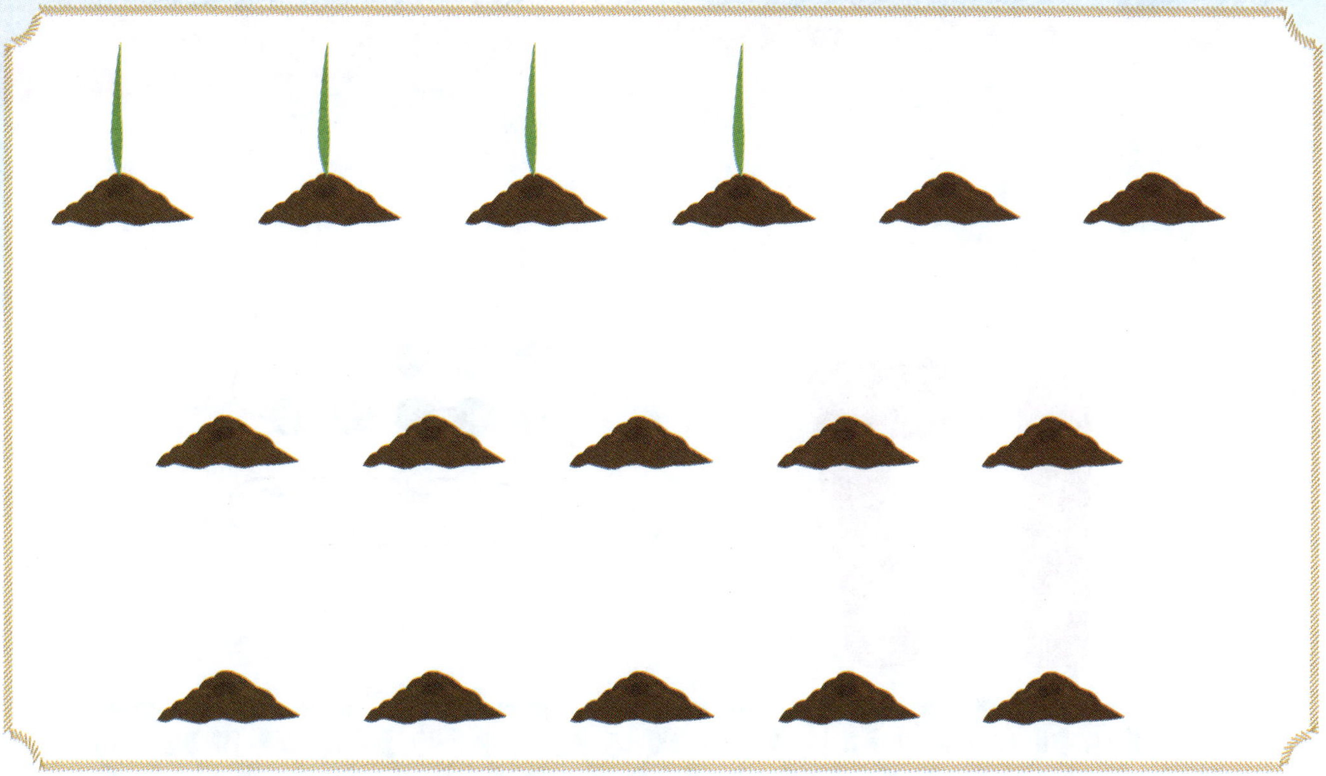

**Trace and write 16.**

| 16 | 16 | 16 | 16 | 16 | 16 |
|---|---|---|---|---|---|
| 16 | 16 | 16 | 16 | 16 | 16 |
| | | | | | |

# HELLO NUMBER 17

**Trace and read.**

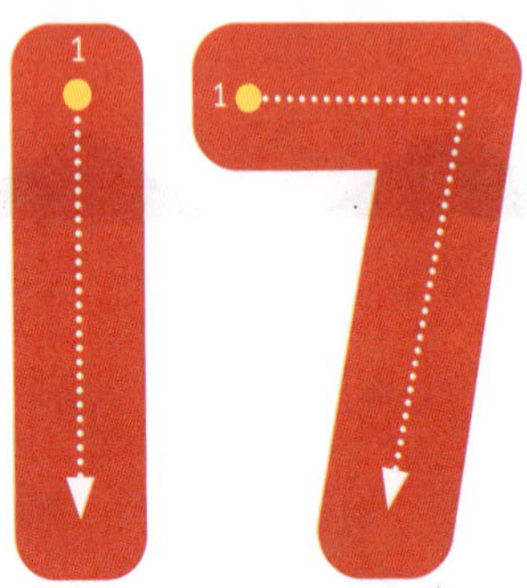

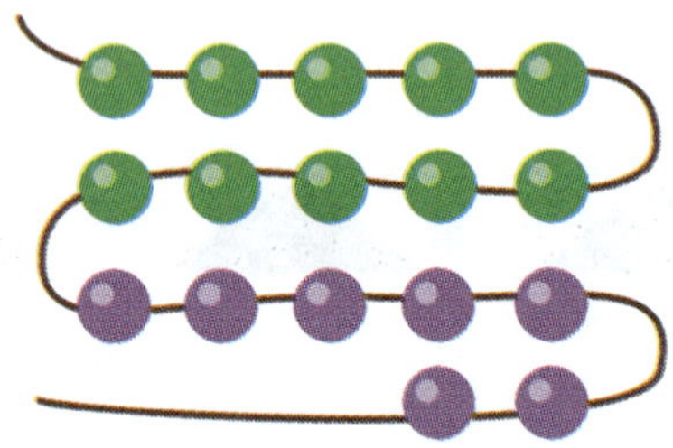

**Draw more triangles so that there are 17 triangles in all.**

**Draw more ice-cream candies so that there are 17 candies in all.**

**Trace and write 17.**

# HELLO NUMBER 18

**Trace and read.**

18

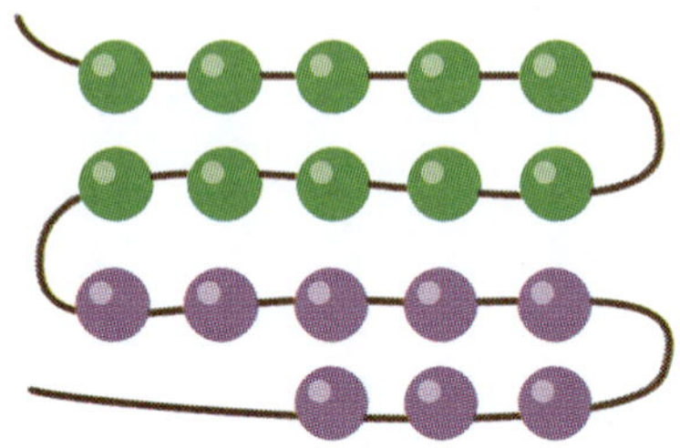

9 10 11 12 13 14 15 16 17 18 19 20

**Draw and colour 18 kites in the space below.**

**Draw more cups so that there are 18 cups in all.**

**Trace and write 18.**

# HELLO NUMBER 19

Trace and read.

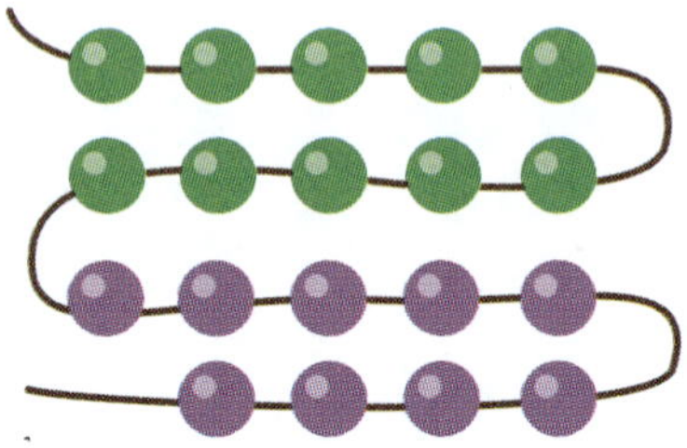

9 10 11 12 13 14 15 16 17 18 19 20

Draw and colour 19 snowflakes in the space below.

Draw more balloons so that there are 19 balloons in all.

Trace and write 19.

# HELLO NUMBER 20

Trace and read.

20

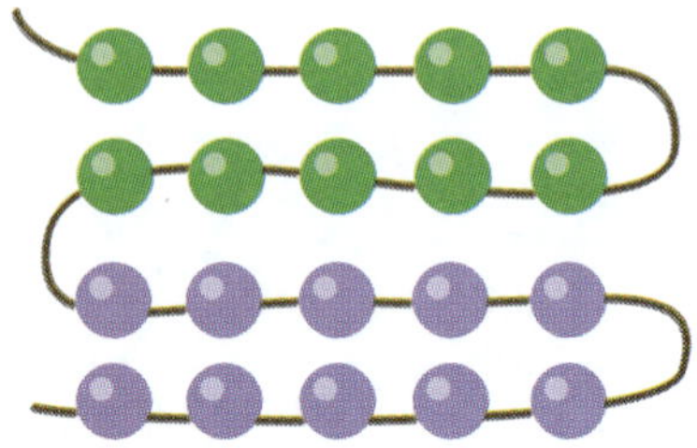

9 10 11 12 13 14 15 16 17 18 19 20

Draw and colour 20 bricks in the space below.

**Draw more clouds so that there are 20 clouds in all.**

**Trace and write 20.**

# I KNOW!

Trace and write the numbers.

| | | | | |
|---|---|---|---|---|
| 16 | 16 | 16 | 16 | |
| 17 | 17 | 17 | 17 | |
| 18 | 18 | 18 | 18 | |
| 19 | 19 | 19 | 19 | |
| 20 | 20 | 20 | 20 | |

# I KNOW!

Fill in the missing numbers to take the astronaut to the planet.

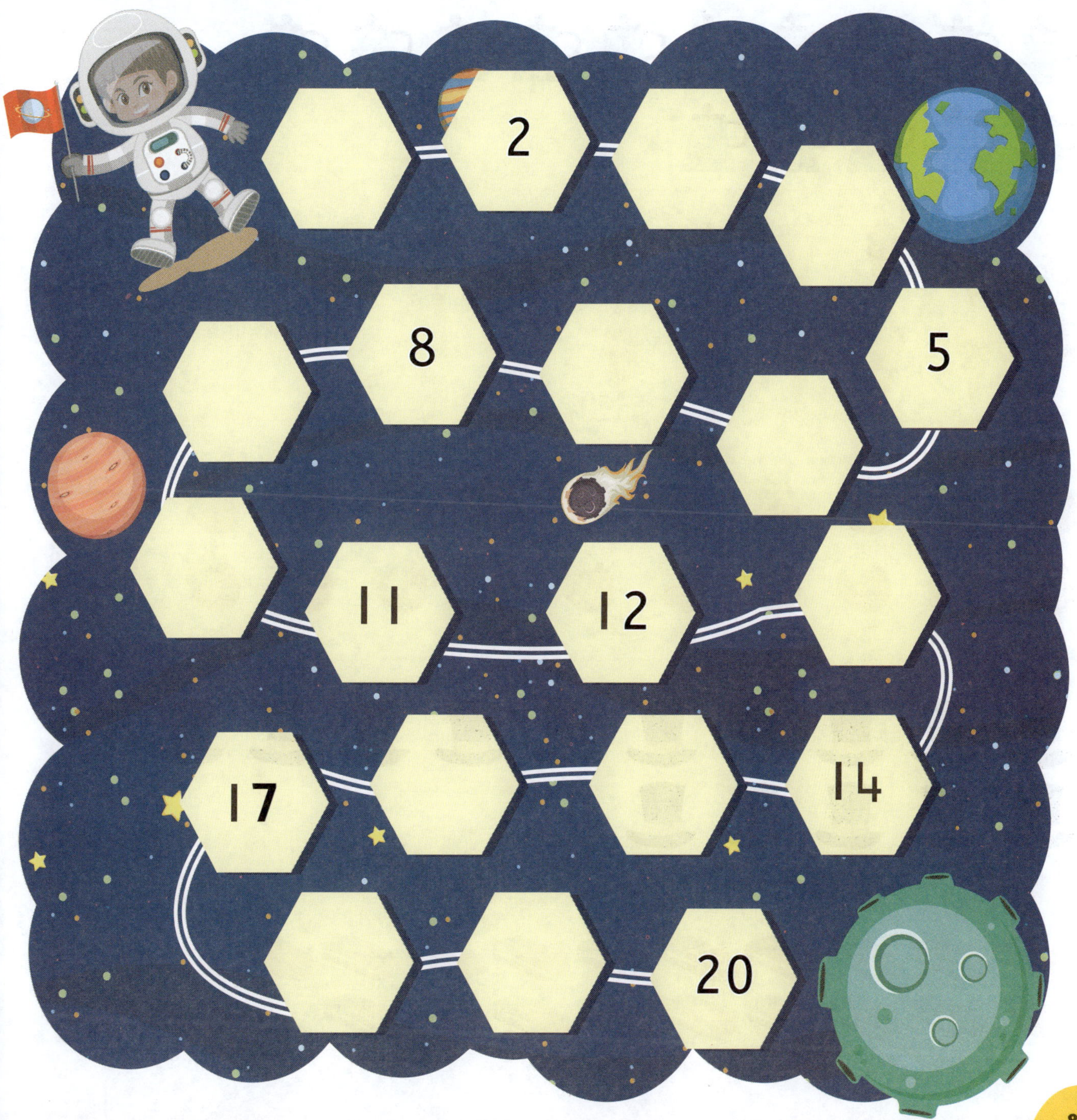

# COUNT AND WRITE

**Count and write the number of objects.**

# BACKWARD COUNTING 20-1

# BEFORE-AFTER-BETWEEN

Write the numbers that come just before.

Write the numbers that come just after.

Write the missing number between the given numbers.

# MORE-LESS

Ring the set with more coins.

Look at the picture. Tick (✓) which object appears more.

☐

☐

# NUMBER NAMES 1-20

Trace and write.

| | |
|---|---|
| 1 | one |
| 2 | two |
| 3 | three |
| 4 | four |
| 5 | five |

one

two

three

four

five

## Trace and write.

| Number | Word | Trace | Write |
|---|---|---|---|
| 6 | six | six | |
| 7 | seven | seven | |
| 8 | eight | eight | |
| 9 | nine | nine | |
| 10 | ten | ten | |

11 12 13 14 15 16 17 18 19 20

## Trace and write.

| | | | |
|---|---|---|---|
| 11 | eleven | eleven | |
| 12 | twelve | twelve | |
| 13 | thirteen | thirteen | |
| 14 | fourteen | fourteen | |
| 15 | fifteen | fifteen | |

**Trace and write.**

| | | |
|---|---|---|
| 16 | sixteen | sixteen |
| 17 | seventeen | seventeen |
| 18 | eighteen | eighteen |
| 19 | nineteen | nineteen |
| 20 | twenty | twenty |

# GROUPS OF TEN

**Count and read.**

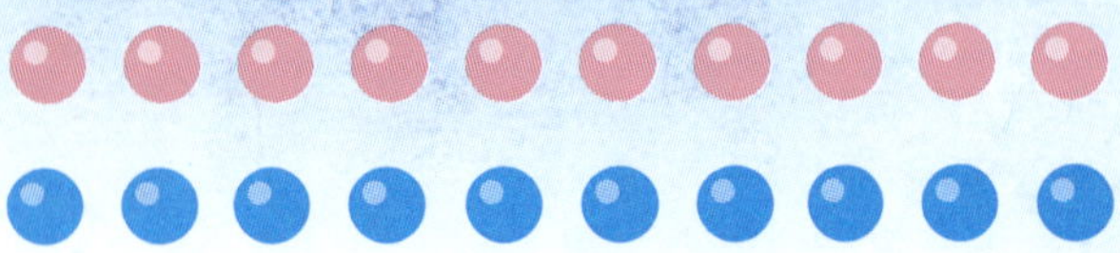

20

Groups of ten

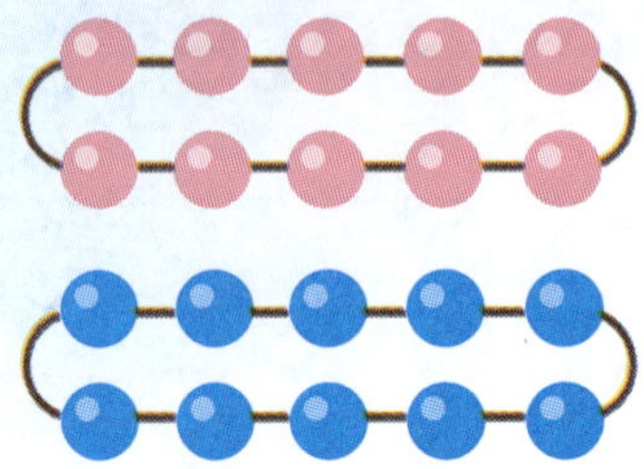

10

10

**Ring the objects in groups of 10. Count and write the number.**

☐

☐

☐

☐

# COUNTING FROM 21-30

15 16 17 18 19 20 21 22 23 24 25 26 27 28 29 30

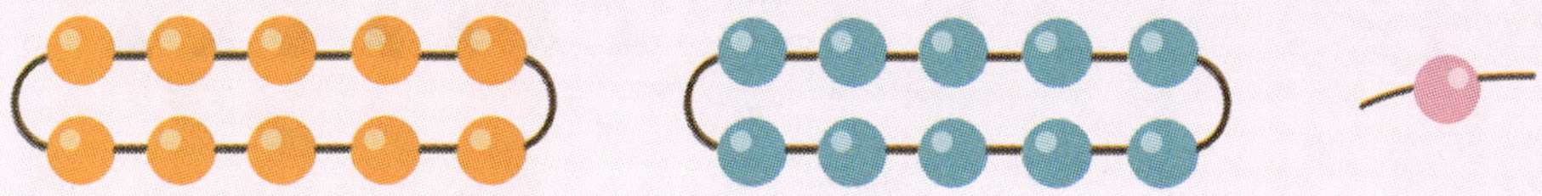

Trace and write.

| | | | | | |
|---|---|---|---|---|---|
| 21 | 26 | 21 | 26 | | |
| 22 | 27 | 22 | 27 | | |
| 23 | 28 | 23 | 28 | | |
| 24 | 29 | 24 | 29 | | |
| 25 | 30 | 25 | 30 | | |

Read, count and trace.

21

21

26

26

22

22

27

27

23

23

28

28

24

24

29

29

25

25

30

30

# COUNTING FROM 31–40

25 26 27 28 29 30 31 32 33 34 35 36 37 38 39 40

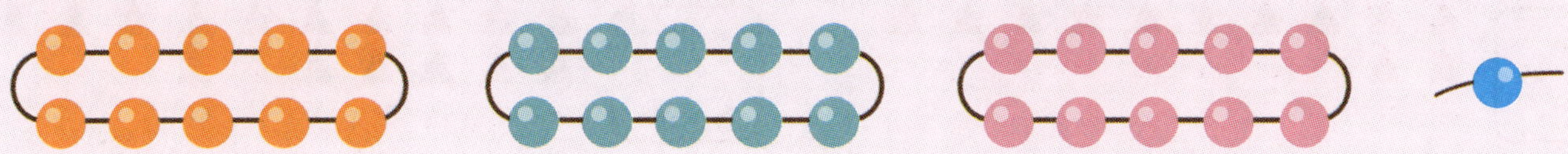

**Trace and write.**

| | | | | | |
|---|---|---|---|---|---|
| 31 | 36 | 31 | 36 | | |
| 32 | 37 | 32 | 37 | | |
| 33 | 38 | 33 | 38 | | |
| 34 | 39 | 34 | 39 | | |
| 35 | 40 | 35 | 40 | | |

## Read, count and trace.

31

31

36

36

32

32

37

37

33

33

38

38

34

34

39

39

35

35

40

40

# COUNTING FROM 41 – 50

35 36 37 38 39 40 41 42 43 44 45 46 47 48 49 50

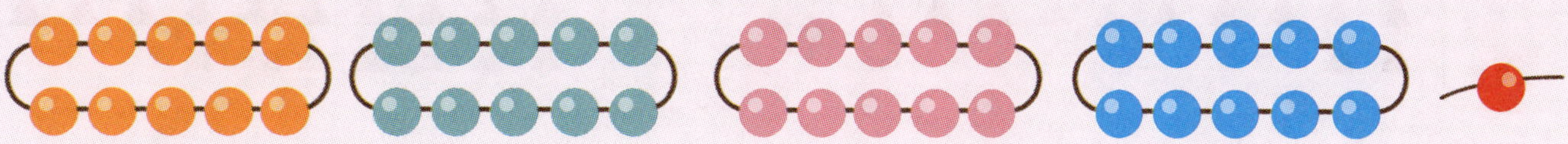

Trace and write.

| | | | | | |
|---|---|---|---|---|---|
| 41 | 46 | 41 | 46 | | |
| 42 | 47 | 42 | 47 | | |
| 43 | 48 | 43 | 48 | | |
| 44 | 49 | 44 | 49 | | |
| 45 | 50 | 45 | 50 | | |

**Read, count and trace.**

41

41

42

42

43

43

44

44

45

45

46

46

47

47

48

48

49

49

50

50



1 2 3 4 5 6 7 8 9 10

# I KNOW!

Count and tick (✓) the correct number.

28 22 24

26 21 25

31 36 39

Count and tick (✓) the correct number.

37 40 34

41 48 45

49 43 46

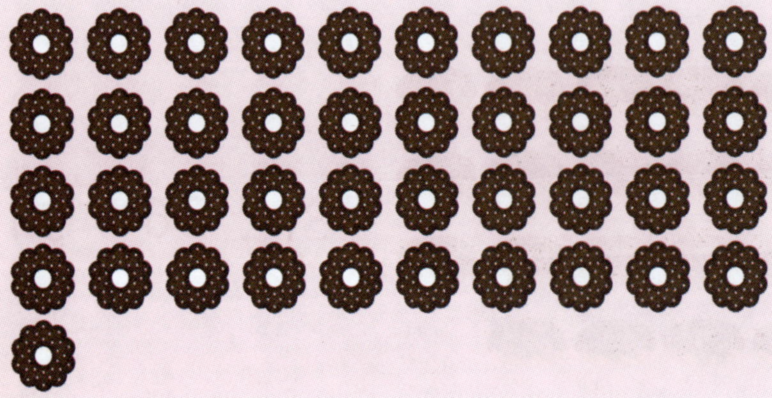

42 44 41

# SKIP COUNTING

**Sing.**

Mr. Kangaroo jumps from 2 to 4, leaving 3 on the floor,
He jumps from 4 to 6, and gives number 5 a miss.
2, 4, 6, 8, 10, and on he goes,
Mr. Kangaroo skips and counts by 2's.

**Paste stickers to show how Mr. Kangaroo jumps.**

# SKIP COUNTING

**Fill in the missing numbers.**

| 1 | | 3 | | 5 | | 7 | |
|---|---|---|---|---|---|---|---|
| | | 13 | | 11 | | 9 | |
| | 15 | | 17 | | 19 | | |

FINISH

**Write the numbers that will come next.**

| | | | | | |
|---|---|---|---|---|---|
| 2 | 4 | 6 | 8 | | |
| 10 | 12 | 14 | | | |
| 3 | 5 | 7 | | | |
| 7 | 9 | | | | |

# COUNTING FROM 51–60

45 46 47 48 49 50 51 52 53 54 55 56 57 58 59 60

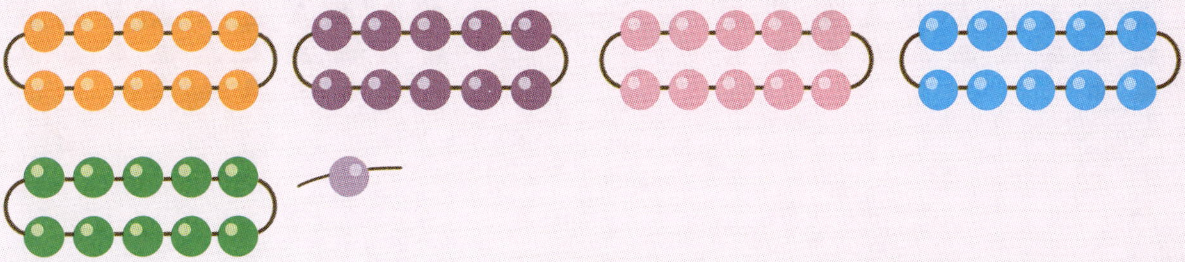

Trace and write.

| | | | | | |
|---|---|---|---|---|---|
| 51 | 56 | 51 | 56 | | |
| 52 | 57 | 52 | 57 | | |
| 53 | 58 | 53 | 58 | | |
| 54 | 59 | 54 | 59 | | |
| 55 | 60 | 55 | 60 | | |

## Read, count and trace.

51

51

52

52

53

53

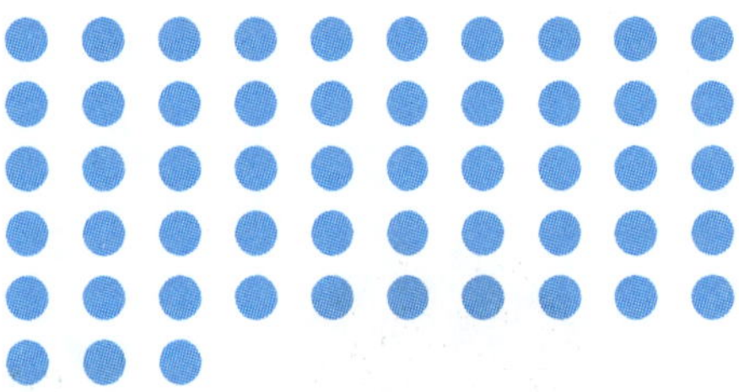

54

54

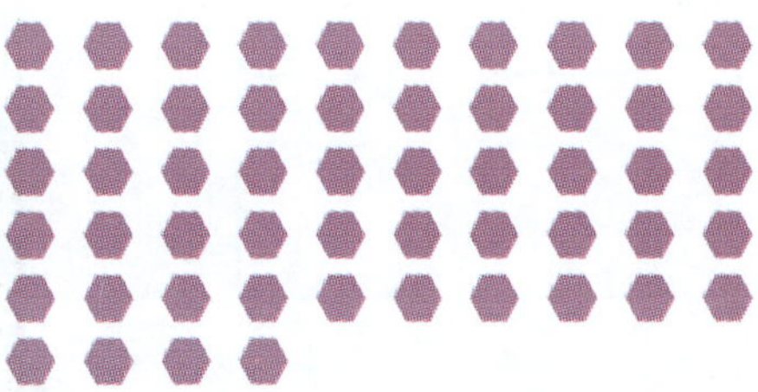

55

55

56

56

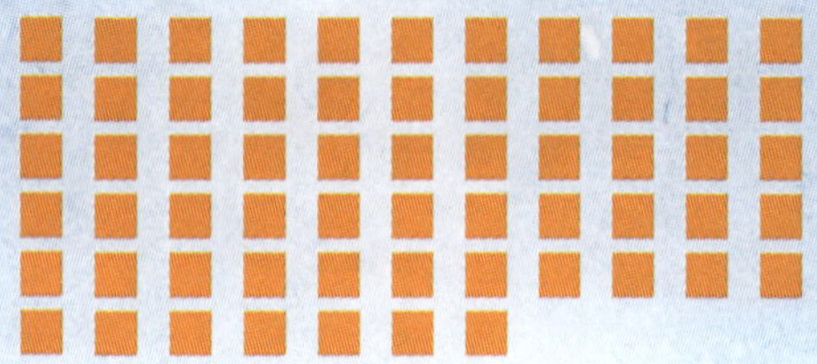

57

57

58

58

59

59

60

60

# COUNTING FROM 61–70

55 56 57 58 59 60 61 62 63 64 65 66 67 68 69 70

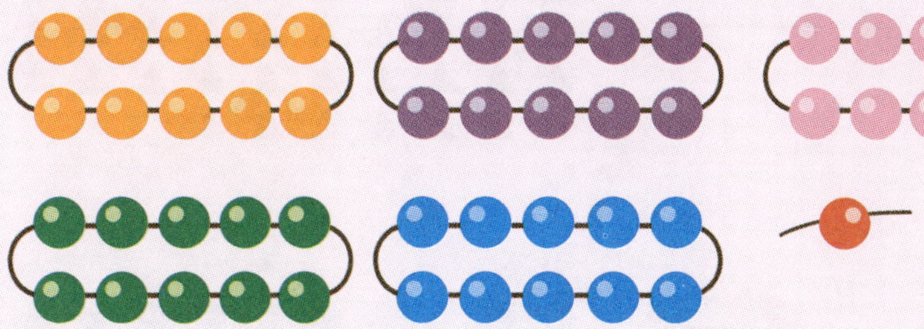

**Trace and write.**

| | | | | | |
|---|---|---|---|---|---|
| 61 | 66 | 61 | 66 | | |
| 62 | 67 | 62 | 67 | | |
| 63 | 68 | 63 | 68 | | |
| 64 | 69 | 64 | 69 | | |
| 65 | 70 | 65 | 70 | | |

## Read, count and trace.

61

61

62

62

63

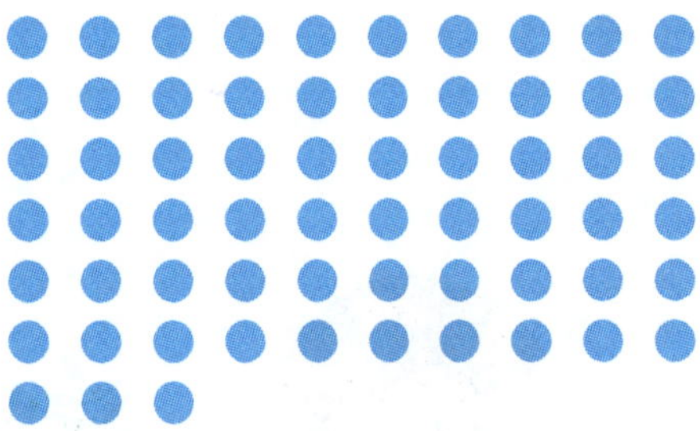

63

64

64

65

65

66

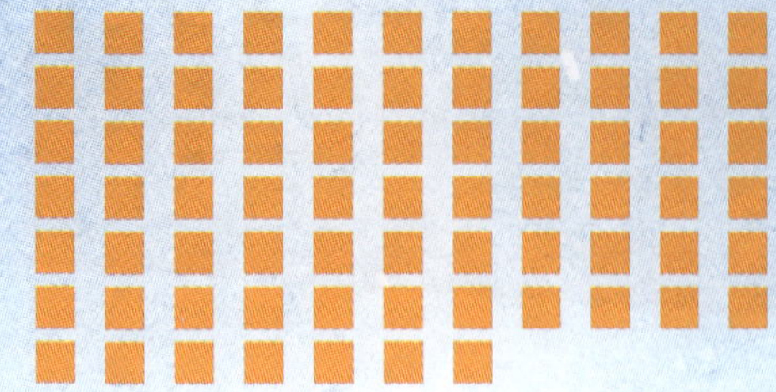

66

67

67

68

68

69

69

70

70

# COUNTING FROM 71–80

65 66 67 68 69 70 71 72 73 74 75 76 77 78 79 80

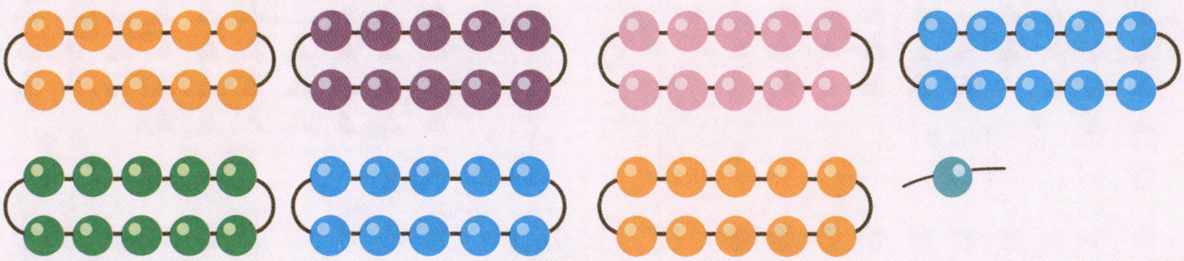

Trace and write.

| | | | | | |
|---|---|---|---|---|---|
| 71 | 76 | 71 | 76 | | |
| 72 | 77 | 72 | 77 | | |
| 73 | 78 | 73 | 78 | | |
| 74 | 79 | 74 | 79 | | |
| 75 | 80 | 75 | 80 | | |

**Read, count and trace.**

71

71

72

72

73

73

74

74

75

75

76

76

77

77

78

78

79

79

80

80

# COUNTING FROM 81–90

75 76 77 78 79 80 81 82 83 84 85 86 87 88 89 90

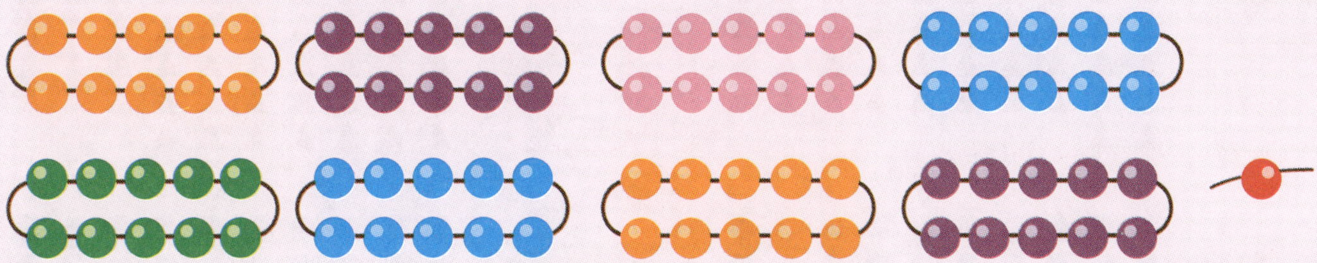

**Trace and write.**

| | | | | | |
|---|---|---|---|---|---|
| 81 | 86 | 81 | 86 | | |
| 82 | 87 | 82 | 87 | | |
| 83 | 88 | 83 | 88 | | |
| 84 | 89 | 84 | 89 | | |
| 85 | 90 | 85 | 90 | | |

## Read, count and trace.

81

81

82

82

83

83

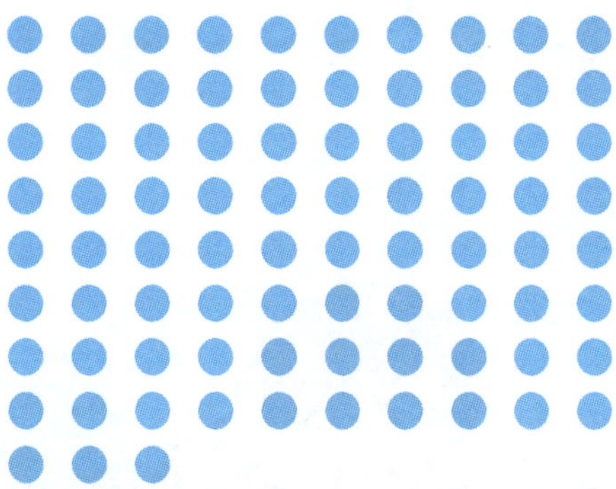

84

84

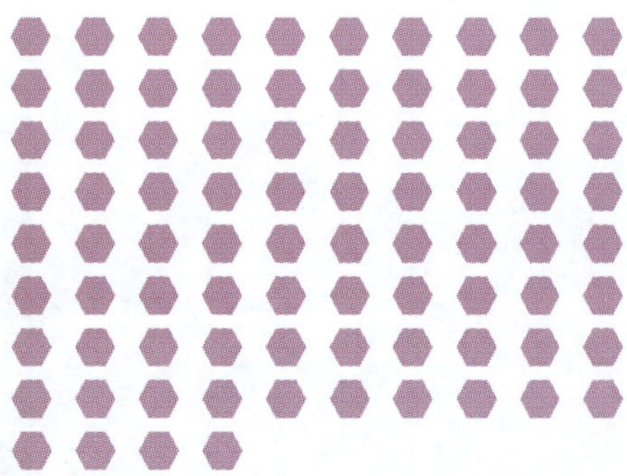

85

85

86

86

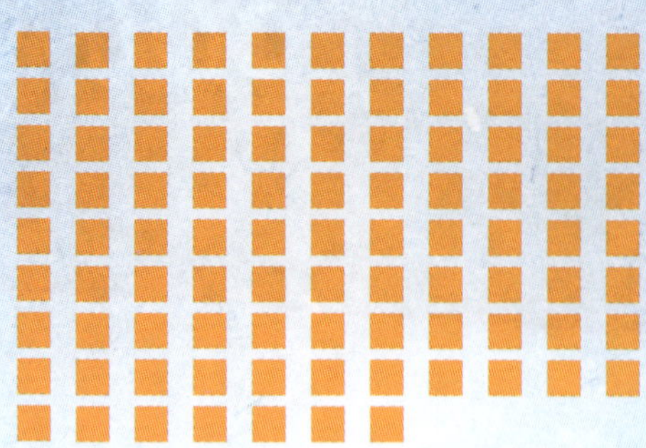

87

87

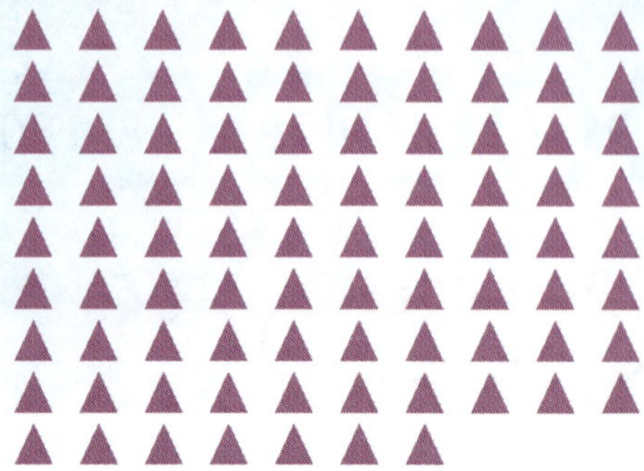

88

88

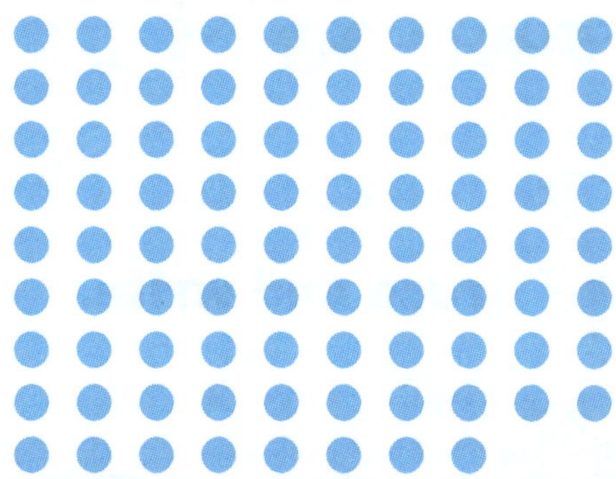

89

89

90

90

# COUNTING FROM 91–100

85 86 87 88 89 90 91 92 93 94 95 96 97 98 99 100

Trace and write.

| | | | | | |
|---|---|---|---|---|---|
| 91 | 96 | 91 | 96 | | |
| 92 | 97 | 92 | 97 | | |
| 93 | 98 | 93 | 98 | | |
| 94 | 99 | 94 | 99 | | |
| 95 | 100 | 95 | 100 | | |

Read, count and trace.

91

91

92

92

93

93

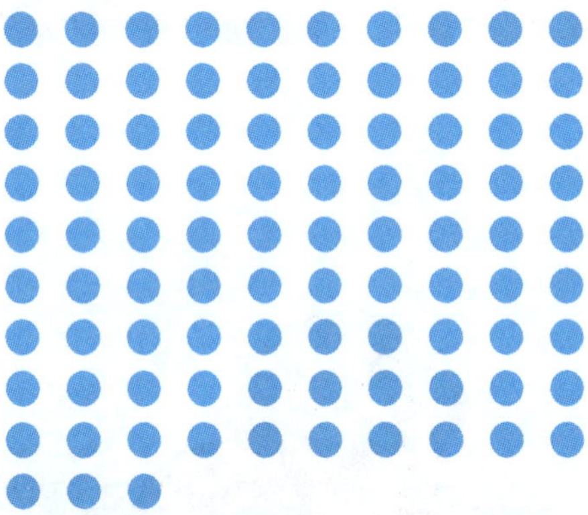

94

94

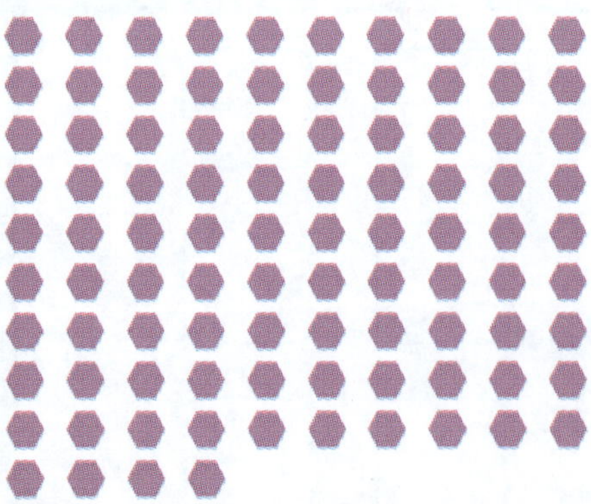

95

95

96

96

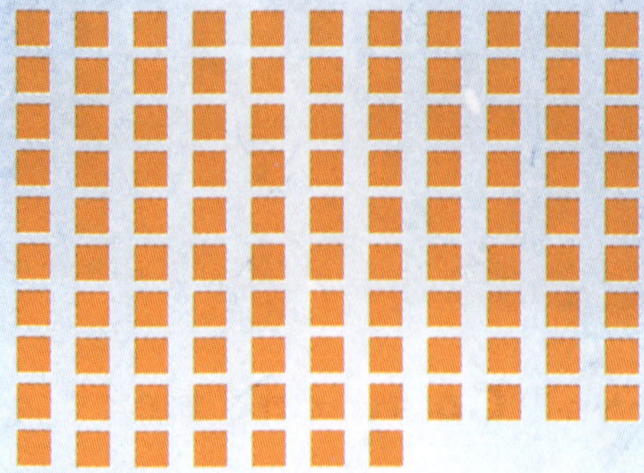

97

97

98

98

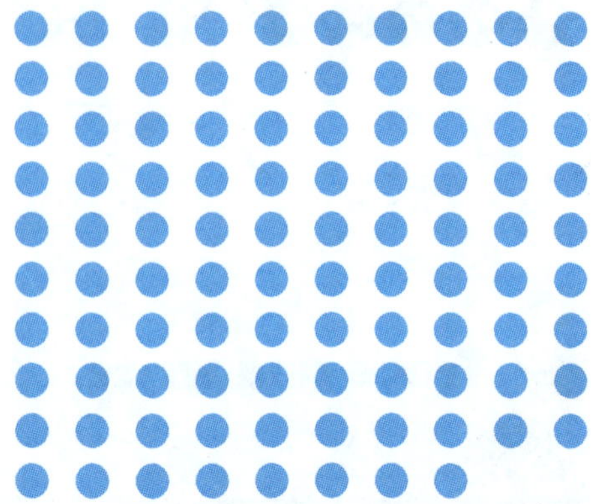

99

99

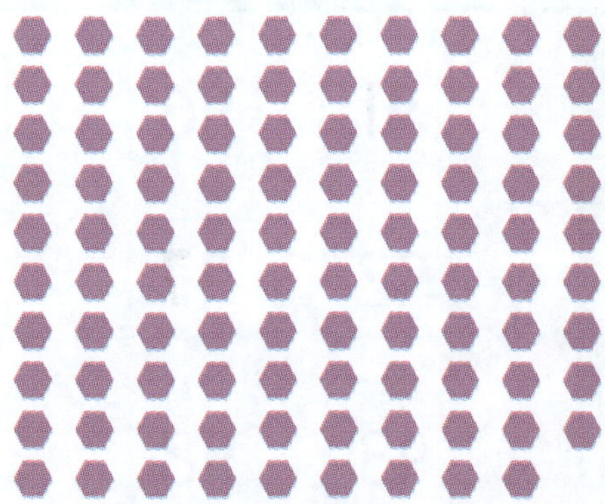

100

100

# I KNOW!

**Count and tick (✓) the correct number.**

51 53 57

68 65 61

72 74 79

## Count and tick (✓) the correct number.

87 81 82

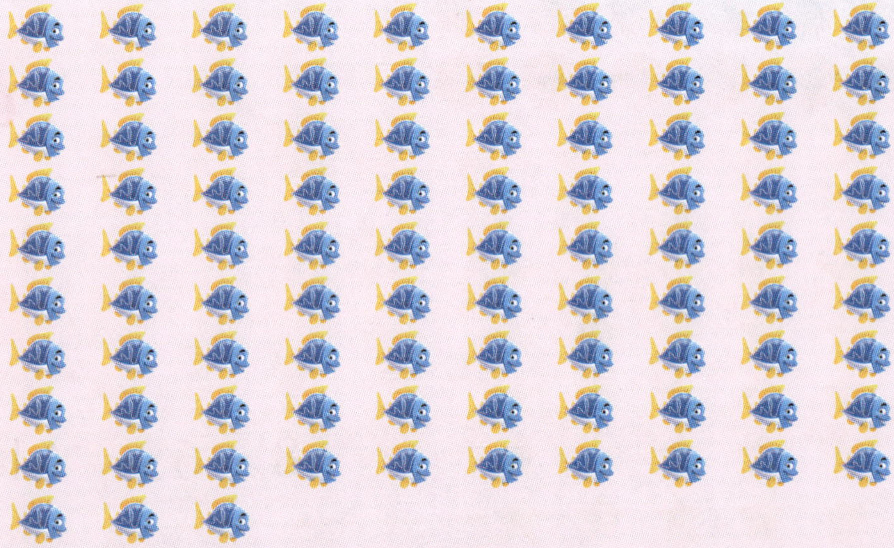

95 93 99

93 95 100

**Page 41:**

**Page 48:**

RELCRO

**Page 56:**

**Page 107:**